Cai~~~~~~

A Concise History, Language, Culture, Cuisine, Transport and Travel Guide

by

Wily World Travelers

© Copyright 2017 by Wily World Travelers
All rights reserved.

The following eBook is reproduced below with the goal of providing information that is as accurate and reliable as possible. Regardless, purchasing this eBook can be seen as consent to the fact that both the publisher and the author of this book are in no way experts on the topics discussed within and that any recommendations or suggestions that are made herein are for entertainment purposes only. Professionals should be consulted as needed prior to undertaking any of the action endorsed herein.

This declaration is deemed fair and valid by both the American Bar Association and the Committee of Publishers Association and is legally binding throughout the United States.

Furthermore, the transmission, duplication or reproduction of any of the following work including specific information will be considered an illegal act irrespective of if it is done electronically or in print. This extends to creating a secondary or tertiary copy of the work or a recorded copy and is only allowed with express written consent from the Publisher. All additional rights reserved.

The information in the following pages is broadly considered to be a truthful and accurate account of facts and as such any inattention, use or misuse of the information in question by the reader will render any resulting actions solely under their purview. There are no scenarios in which the publisher or the original author of this work can be in any fashion deemed liable for any hardship or damages that may befall them after undertaking information described herein.

Additionally, the information in the following pages is intended only for informational purposes and should thus be thought of as universal. As befitting its nature, it is presented without assurance regarding its prolonged validity or interim quality. Trademarks that are mentioned are done without written consent and can in no way be considered an endorsement from the trademark holder.

Table of Contents

Introduction 5

Chapter 1: Enjoying a Rich History and Inspiring Culture 9

Chapter 2: Speaking Their Language 18

Chapter 3: Getting to Know Cambodia through Its Cuisine 28

Chapter 4: Learning to Navigate — Cambodian Style 36

Chapter 5: Destinations You Don't Want to Miss 44

Chapter 6: Celebrating Today's Cambodia 53

Conclusion: 57

Introduction

Today's Cambodia is the result of a past filled with a mysterious mixture of peace and power, chaos and calm. It's a diverse land that offers ancient explorations for the independent spirit, artistic inspiration for those whose dream is to surround themselves with exotic beauty, and spiritual insight for travelers seeking a higher source of wisdom and awareness. Cambodia is a country of extremes, touting lush jungle lowlands and remarkably rugged mountain ranges. One moment you're navigating through the busy streets of the capital city of Phnom Penh, and the next you're cycling through a remote village to be greeted by the friendly locals.

It's easy to miss some of the Cambodian wonders if you don't know where to go or how to get there, which is why this book can be your guide through this amazing Asian adventure. By traveling first through the pages of our book, you'll learn which rivers to kayak, ancient temples and ruins to visit, and trendy nightclubs and restaurants to frequent. You'll also learn some local expressions and favorite phrases to help you communicate—Cambodian style.

Our goal is to create an easy-to-travel roadmap that enables you to experience Cambodia's people and places and become immersed in their customs, culture, and cuisine. Whether your pleasure is to seek solace in the serenity of one of their ancient temples, kayak with the river dolphins, enjoy the grandeur of the Royal Palace, or shop in the modern city of Phnom Penh, you'll find it all in the richly textured layers that make up Cambodia.

Accommodations and food are so affordable that you can extend your stay without it killing your vacation budget for the next year. Choose a luxury hotel in the city for as little as $50 to $75 U.S. dollars a night, or rent an oceanfront vacation home for only $25 a night. As reasonable as their prices are, their hospitality is outrageous—first-class all the way. There are two seasons in Cambodia: wet and dry. From November to May is considered their dry season, which is a much more comfortable time to visit than their rainy season from June to October. However, no matter what season you're there, you can always find a street-side vendor willing to mix up a refreshing pineapple or banana smoothie to quench your thirst and revive you for the afternoon's activities.

When you need a cooling off, you can soak up some sunshine and take a dip in the crystal-clear waters on one of the pristine beaches of Sihanoukville. Since it's become a world-class destination, don't be surprised to hear several languages being spoken by the people in the next hammock over. Cambodia's displayed history, beautiful architecture, and smiling citizens is no longer a well-kept secret. They are proud of their robust tourist industry, which can be evidenced by the warm and inviting welcomes of villagers and retailers alike.

If you're an animal lover, Cambodia has a myriad of amazing wild and domesticated animals. The Asian Golden Cat is one that lives in the wilds of the jungle. It is between the sizes of a large domestic cat and a smaller leopard. Cambodians hold this cat in high regard, believing it to have mystical protective powers for those hiking or horseback riding through the dense forest regions. As you travel through the countryside, it's common to see water buffalo working the rice fields to help the villagers plow and harvest. Deeper in the jungle, you'll hear the chatter of monkeys and the call of their various species of exotic birds. And, of course, the Asian Elephant is king of all.

Don't pack just yet, but when you do take our book along with you and use it as your guide. Also, don't forget to pack a camera. You'll want to capture your memories for all your friends back home. Most of all, take your innate curiosity, your high expectations, and your childlike wonderment as you visit one of the most intriguing vacation destinations in the world—Cambodia.

Chapter 1: Enjoying a Rich History and Inspiring Culture

With its neighboring countries of Vietnam, Laos, and Thailand, it's evident that much of Cambodia's historical and architectural influences have come from these countries. However, much of Cambodia's religious rites and political practices have been borrowed from the East Indian beliefs of Hinduism and Buddhism as well. Many of Cambodia's massive temples, ceremonial customs, and unique artistic expressions in dance and music were developed from the 9th to the 14th century, which was known as their golden age.

Like many other prosperous empires of Southeast Asia, regional wars and royal family feuds caused societal collapse. This left Cambodia and much of its prized national treasures in decay and ruin until the French Colonials began to rule in 1863. Fierce fighting and radical societal changes continued, peaking when the Communist Party of Kampuchea overpowered the Khmer Republic. With these changes, the people suffered terrible atrocities by the governing powers, and most of the country's educators, business leaders, artists, and high-ranking officials were murdered during the civil war between 1975 and 1979.

Between those murdered and the ones who later died of starvation and disease, the number of deaths was estimated to be well over a million citizens. Because of the Communist Khmer Rouge, Cambodia's most valued temple of Angkor was threatened, which would have meant a significant historical and cultural loss for all its people. Finally, in 1991, a peace agreement was initiated, and international organizations pooled their resources to assist the Cambodian Government in restoring its sites and rebuilding its cities.

It has been a long and exhausting struggle for Cambodia to reinstate its repressed religious and educational systems and re-establish a secure financial center and business community, but today Cambodia is enjoying the fruits of its labor. Its villages tout prosperous rice cultivation, a growing fishing industry, and animal husbandry, while it's cities benefit from the growing tourist trade and retail development.

Typical Cambodian Lifestyle

Most of rural Cambodia is occupied by smaller farming communities, where the people live in modest homes built of wood and covered by quaint thatched roofs. Bamboo walls divide the inside rooms, and the food preparation and cooking is done in a small kitchen located behind the main house. Many of the homes are raised six to ten feet off the ground to avoid the high waters brought by the rains during the wet season.

Looking across the dozens and dozens of floating rice fields, it's common to see the water buffalo pulling a hand-held plow and men and women in their large, straw hats planting behind. Chores are fairly divided among all members of the family, with both men and women working in the fields and sharing the household duties as well. When children have reached the ages of eight to ten years, they are expected to work alongside their parents. If they have been chosen to attend the monastery, which is a great honor by their parents, the children will be educated by the monks and live among them for extended periods.

Life in urban Cambodia is quite different, with shopkeepers and café owners educating their children and teaching them to assume the duties of the family business. Equally as important as learning to read and write, are their lessons in religion and fine arts. At an early age, Cambodian children learn religion, dance, music, and theater, with an emphasis on their national history and artistic treasures.

Cambodian Religions and Social Customs

Approximately 80 percent of Cambodians are Buddhist, with the rest of the population practicing Islam, atheism, animism, and a small percentage of Christians. Since the persecution of Khmer Islam during the rule of Khmer Rouge, Islam's numbers have dwindled. Although the Roman Catholics introduced Christianity in the 1660s, there has been very little increase in their numbers as well, estimating them to make up less than one percent of the total population. The animists, or tribesmen who worship invisible spirits associated with water, fire, and earth, consist of about 100,000 people.

There is a great respect for the aged in Cambodia, with particular words to address them that show high regard and politeness. Parents are the authority in the households, showing strictness and expecting obedience from the younger generation. Children live with their parents until they marry, and premarital relations are forbidden. Some parents still choose spouses for their daughters, but, for the most part, girls are given the opportunity to renounce their decision. Most important for all parties in the selection process is family status and reputation.

Wedding ceremonies are long, luxurious affairs, with elaborate gowns, jewelry, the lighting of beautiful candles, and many blessings and well-wishes from family and friends. After the wedding, the bride and groom are then expected to live with the wife's family until they earn enough money to build a home nearby. Marriages in Cambodia are more than a legal contract; they are socially-supported unions, and couples that do not respect their vows are chastised and held in low regard.

Cambodians believe that their souls are contained in their heads, making it unacceptably rude to touch another's head or point your feet at someone's head. Feet are believed to be lowly and impure, and it is disrespectful to use your feet to kick or point to a person or to direct another.

The respectful way to greet those of Cambodia is to assume the "sampeah" posture, which looks much like one involved in humble prayer. The hands are pressed before the chest, the head is slightly bowed, and the eyes do not meet. In fact, it is considered impolite for a younger person to meet the eyes of their elders, who are to be thought of as their superiors. Also, when sitting in a chair, the legs should not be crossed. Again, that is a sign of impoliteness. From early childhood, Cambodian's are taught that good manners and confident temperaments are evidenced by a gentle manner and quiet disposition.

The Cambodian Dress

One of the most memorable elements of Cambodian culture is the distinctive dress of its people. It's easy to identify the status and ethnicity of the individuals of Cambodia because their clothing sets them apart. For example, Khmer people wear a traditional "karma," which is a checkered scarf that you will not see worn by the Thais, Vietnamese or the people of Laos. You will often see the royal caste Cambodians dressed in a beautifully decorated cape called a "shai" or "rabai kanorng" across the left shoulder. The wealthier the person, the more silver and gold they will have sewn into the fabric to make it glimmer and shine with every movement.

Headdresses that resemble tiaras are also worn by the upper-class Cambodian woman, which are similar to those we see on the heads of classical Asian dancers. The colorful fabrics of their dress are softly folded across the body, wrapping around the woman's body to complement her feminine form. Both males and females wear the boldly colored sarongs, lightly looped around their legs and tucked at the waist. It's also common to see men wearing formal jackets with bold colors and elaborate designs while accentuating their shoulders with heavy padding.

Of course, with the more Westernized dress and styles coming to Cambodia, and visiting tourists from all over the world, almost any type of dress is acceptable. Keep in mind as you pack your own clothing, the weather is rather hot and humid, so include clothes that breathe and insulate your body. While you're there, you'll probably be tempted to adapt to the Cambodian dress and wear the lighter fabrics that move with the slightest of breezes to cool the skin and allow greater freedom of movement.

Cambodian Music and Dance

The classical dance of Cambodia used to be reserved for only the royalty, but this has changed as the tourists have come to appreciate the grace and beauty of its dancers. The hands and feet of the dancers are used to express emotions, and their choreography tells the religious and mythical stories of old. While the classical dancers represent Royals, the folk dancers tell a different story. Their costumes depict farmers and peasants, and a mahori orchestra plays the music. This is an ensemble which consists of only three people: a singer, a Saw sam sai, and a drummer, the drum being like those used in China or Tibet. It's fast-paced movements, and joyful designs have become a hit with travelers as well as the locals.

During festivals or special events, the music and dance is a mixture of classical and folk. Musical instruments are mostly percussion types, gongs, and reeds. Cambodia's music is as transparent and authentic as its dance, dress, and people, representing a changing tide in its communities. With the onslaught of Westernization that has bridged the Cambodian culture to that of the West, it's obvious they have been just as interested in the travelers' shared music and dance as we have with their performances.

The Cambodian's Ancient Arts

When it comes to their artistic expressions, there is almost nothing Western about it. When you visit their incredible temples and extensive ancient ruins, you are taken into the past; a past filled with spiritual beings and stone carvings that depict people steeped in religion, war, and mythical beings and beliefs. Although the Khmer Rouge rid the country of most of their artists, the 21st century is seeing a return to its first love, displaying a real revival of the arts. We'll discuss more of the arts as we guide you through Cambodia's ancient temples and ruins.

Now that you're getting a bit of the flavor of Cambodia, you'll want to know how to speak the language of its people, both in mannerisms and voice. In the next chapter, we'll talk about the spoken and unspoken ways to communicate with the Cambodian people.

Chapter 2: Speaking Their Language

Many of us, especially Americans, expect people of other countries to speak English, and we travel abroad with those same unreasonable expectations. In fact, we are often surprised when English is not understood, or when we are expected to speak the language of the people we are visiting. When they come to our country, we expect them to be fluent in English. Unfortunately, we have adopted a double standard when it comes to traveling outside the country. So, to make your visit to Cambodia better, we have given you some common phrases, gestures, and body language to learn that will help to make your stay more comfortable and less offensive.

Approximately 95 percent of Cambodians speak Khmer. To learn Khmer is difficult, since it has one of the largest alphabets, with 23 vowels, 12 independent vowels, and 33 consonants. However, the Cambodian language is a bit easier to understand as it is not tonal, meaning the word meaning doesn't change with the difference in high or low pitch of the word or sound. Although it will be helpful to know some common phrases, you can rest assured that many of the people of Cambodia are fluent in English, especially in the larger cities like Phnom Penh, Siem Reap, and Kompong Som. The older and more elite Cambodians also speak French and Mandarin.

Learning Useful Cambodian Phrases

The following words and phrases will help you when you are greeting others.

Hello	jumreap sooa
Where are you from?	Niak mao pi patet nah?
How are you?	Tau neak sok sapbaiy jea the?
What is your name?	lok tch muoh ey?
Please	sohm Mehta
Thank you	orgoon
Good morning	arun suor sdei
Good afternoon	tiveah suor sdei
Good evening	sayoanh suor sdei
Goodnight	reahtrey suor sdei
Yes	baat
No	dteh
Goodbye	leah suhn heuy

Note: When addressing a man by name, it is polite to say "Lok," then follow that with his first name and surname. When addressing a woman, you say "Lok Srey," then follow with her first name and surname.

Note: Since Cambodians are a hierarchy society when greeting someone of higher rank than you, you should bow lower and avoid making eye contract. Also, when you press your hands together as if praying, the higher ranking the person with whom you are greeting, the higher your hands should be on your chest.

Note: When you are talking to a person that is higher ranking than yourself, you should give them space. Make it a habit of standing at least three feet away from them.

Note: Many Cambodians have adopted the habit of shaking hands when greeting Americans, so it's important to accept any type of greeting that is offered. Be careful not to squeeze their hand too firmly, as this could be misconstrued as a show of aggression.

Note: When being introduced to others, keep in mind the one with the highest ranking will be introduced first. You should do the same, so there is no confusion for the Cambodians.

When you are asking directions, or need to find the desired transportation, you will find these words and phrases helpful.

Turn right	bawt s´dum
Turn left	bawt ch´weng
Go straight on	teuv trawng
Where is...?	Noev eah nah...?
Hotel	sohnthakia
Car	laan
Toilet	bawngkohn
Bus	laan ch´nout
Boat	dtook
Train	roht plerng
Cyclo	see kola
Aeroplane	yohn hawh

When you want to communicate times and days, these words will come in handy.

Sunday	t´ngai bpoot
Monday	t´ngai jan
Tuesday	t´ngai onggeea
Wednesday	t´ngai bpoot
Thursday	t´ngai bprahoaa
Friday	t´ngai sao
Today	t´ngai nih

Tomorrow	t´ngai saaik
Yesterday	m´werl menh
Morning	bpreuk
Afternoon	r´sial
Evening	l´ngiat

Knowing how to count to ten will be necessary, especially when you need to pay for something or set an appointment.

One	moo ay
Two	bpee
Three	bey
Four	buon
Five	bpram
Six	bpram moo ay
Seven	bpram bpee
Eight	bpram bey
Nine	bpram buon
Ten	dahp

If you and shopping or going to a restaurant, keep these words in mind.

Restaurant	hang bai
I want a ...	k´nyom jang baan ...
Tea	dtai
Sugar	sko
Chicken	moan
Pork	saich jruk
Beef	saich koh
Fish	dt´ray

How much is ...?	t´lay pohnmaan...?
Eat	bpisah
Market	p´sah

Note: Table manners are very important to Cambodians. The oldest person is usually seated first and begins to eat first.

Note: Avoid discussing business while eating. It is meant to be a time for getting to know one another and is considered rude to talk shop.

Practicing Cambodian Etiquette

If you are invited to dinner at someone's home, it is customary to give a small gift of appreciation. However, it is considered rude to open the gift in the presence of the giver. The same holds true if you are given a gift; avoid opening it in the presence of the giver. Gifts are always wrapped in colorful paper—not white. White is the color of mourning, so you can see why it would be inappropriate for gift giving. When you don't know the people well who have invited you to their home, a good gift to give would be flowers or sweets, fruit or pastries. Never give a knife as a gift.

You will never have to worry about what to get a Cambodian for their birthday because unlike us, they do not celebrate birthdays. In fact, many Cambodians couldn't even tell you the date of their birth. Another time of gift giving is during the Cambodian New Year. Remember, when you give a gift, don't hand it to them with your left hand. Present it to them by holding it out with both hands, and accompanied with a slight bow of respect and appreciation for their friendship.

Even business cards are presented in this way—almost as if you were giving your co-worker a gift. When you are introduced to them, you can hand them your business card as if you were presenting a gift with both hands. Business cards are treated with great respect. A thoughtful thing to do would be to have a Khmer translation printed on the back of the card. When you present your card, it should be given with the information facing the Cambodian. You will be judged on how you present your business card, so take the time to do it the right way—with courtesy and politeness.

Personal Conduct

The challenges occur if you are doing business in Cambodia, and your expectations are not being met. Unlike workers in the United States, if Cambodians disagree with you, they will usually remain silent instead of voicing their opposing opinions. It is considered rude to do so. So, if you are conducting a meeting and suddenly the room goes silent, you can assume that there is probably some difference of opinions.

Punctuality is extremely important to Cambodians. Even being five minutes late can show an extreme lack of respect. Whether it is for a casual dinner out or a business meeting, being punctual is key to good relationships. In a culture where modesty and humility are engendered, people who are louder than life or boastful are looked down upon and considered to have bad manners. If one shows emotions, it is seen as a weakness in character. These emotions include anger, frustration, or hurt. One is encouraged to keep their feelings to themselves and work it out another way rather than share with a group.

If one of your subordinates has not lived up to your standards, it's best to bring this up gently and in private. Cambodians make a big deal out of saving face, and anything that could be considered criticism of their work or ethics would make them lose face. Should this happen, it will take much public praise to reverse the damage that has been done and help them to save face once again.

In the United States, when there is a work meeting, we are all eager to get down to business. This is not the case in Cambodia. There must be a time for polite questions about family and personal health and well-being before any business can be discussed. This is a show of respect, and to skip this formality would signal to a Cambodia a disregard for their feelings and a bluntness on your part. Remember, you are dealing with people who have been brought up to believe that the way to resolve a problem is to gently consult with another and wait for them to contribute to the resolution. Nothing is rushed, and anger is suppressed, giving the other person a chance to save face themselves and correct the issue.

A Matter of Dress

Even though Cambodians are becoming more used to foreigners with casual dress and attitudes, you will still be more respected when you adhere to their practices. For this reason, you should always try to dress neatly and honor their customs. When you enter a home or a temple, remove your shoes. Women should wear clothing that covers their shoulders, as bare shoulders are considered suggestive in Cambodian culture. Tank tops, tight t-shirts, and short shorts are frowned upon when worn in public. Men who visit the temples should wear long pants, shirts, and maintain a quiet disposition, always conscious that they are entering a holy place where the gods of the Cambodian ancestors reside.

As you mingle with the people of Cambodia, understand that their customs and beliefs are the results of hundreds of years of teachings, stories, practices, and mandates. As a guest in their country, if you make a mistake they will be too polite to call you on it, but it will be noticed and remembered. It is your responsibility to learn and adopt the Cambodian customs when traveling there. When you do, that too will be noticed and remembered.

Chapter 3: Getting to Know Cambodia through Its Cuisine

There are many television shows out now that have allowed us to experience countries by visiting their restaurants and street vendors to get an idea of their local specialties. Each country has staples and spices that are unique to their locations, but Cambodia is quite different. Why? Its people have been influenced by so many different cultures and ruled by several countries that each time the Cambodians assumed the best of each one, including the wonderful flavors in their cuisine. It isn't unusual to find dishes that have spices similar to those of the Vietnamese, Thai, Chinese, French, and India. There's food to please even the pickiest of palates.

If you have ever eaten Thai or Vietnamese food, you have an inkling of some of the flavors of Khmer cuisine. The food even looks much like what you would get at a Thai restaurant, with lots of noodles, rice, soups, and stir fry. However, as you bite into some of the Cambodian foods, you will notice some distinct flavors that were missing in Thai and Chinese. Those that you might be tasting could be the unique flavors of anise, or the sweet taste of nutmeg and cinnamon. The Cambodian chefs also use available ingredients like kaffir lime leaves, galangal, lemongrass, and shallots to give each dish its Cambodian signature. If you just love Thai food, you may need to add a bit more spices to create more heat in the dishes, as Cambodian foods are not quite as spicy hot.

Like its people, Cambodian food is more gently spiced, more smoothly blended to create subtle mixtures that go well with one another. You will also enjoy the dishes that have been borrowed from China, such as the pork broth rice noodle soup. If you want to kick up the heat, then you can ask that they use some of the many curries from India. It's a safe bet that they will always have Indian curries well-stocked in their kitchens.

Most Cambodians prepare a four-course meal that taps all your taste buds, with savory, sweet, bitter, and salty. Because they are a land with many rivers, fish is readily available and can be found in many of their dishes, from fish soup broth to fermented fish paste, to spicy grilled fish as a main course. Depending on whether you are eating a sweet dish for desert or having it as a side to your main course, sticky or jasmine rice is among the favorites.

In many of their sauces and deserts, the French influence is evident as well. However, where you will get a taste of the French is when patronizing their street vendors as they serve up their yummy baguettes. They are always fresh and crisp, and they are fantastic as a mid-morning snack when cycling around the city. Of course, to quench your thirst, you can almost always find that same vendor ready to prepare a fresh fruit smoothie for you as well. My mouth is watering just thinking about it. The most common fruits of Cambodia are:

| Dragon Fruit | Bananas | Pineapples |
| Watermelon | Mangoes | Jackfruit |

As you shop the outdoor markets, you will also smell the Cambodian delights, especially the Amok. Amok is a fish that has been cooked in coconut milk and wrapped in a banana leaf to be further steamed in chili and special spices. These are offered in many of the street side cafes and open markets. They are eaten like we would eat a taco purchased from the local food truck.

Just a quick few bites and all that's left is the flavorful memory that lingers in your mouth.

What beats all the uptown restaurants that offer a wide variety of wonderful food is the banquet you'll see during Pchum Ben Day (Ancestor's Day). During this day of celebration, Cambodians bring an array of food, flowers, and gifts to the pagoda as a gift to give to the monks. The monks, in turn, make an offering to the gods so that the Cambodians' dead ancestors will not come back to haunt them.

Another time of feasting is during the Khmer New Year or Chaul Chnam Thmey. This festival lasts about three or four days, and it is filled with rituals, dancing, and an delicious feast. In between the lavishly decorated dishes, you will see families playing traditional games and enjoying their new year's celebration for people of all ages.

Of course, it is always a very good time to visit Cambodia, but during the Water Festival you can also taste a variety of mouth-watering food, view the incredibly decorated and lighted boats, listen to the traditional music, and watch dance and fireworks. The Water Festival celebrates the end of the monsoon season, so much of the festival takes place close to the water with boat races and elaborately decorated boats. Be prepared for the crowds, though, because it's such a popular celebration that thousands of people come flooding into the bigger cities to join in the fun.

Most of the restaurants in the larger cities accept credit cards, but as you travel through the countryside, you'll need to pay in Cambodian money. Make sure you have plenty of smaller bills because most of the meals will be quite inexpensive and many of the privately-owned cafes will not have change. Even in the larger cities, you can eat an entire meal for as little as $4. Smoothies, big beers, and street snacks like those baguettes we spoke of can be purchased for well under $1.

To protect your tummies from unwanted upsets, make sure you don't drink tap water or even put ice in your drinks that have not been filtered. Also, when eating fruit, stick to the kind that is protected by a thicker skin, and peel it before eating. Many of the street vendors in the larger cities use precautions in their smoothies, but just ask the hotel staff, and they'll be sure to advise you of which ones to visit.

There are ATMs available in the larger cities as well, but they won't be located on every corner as they are in the States. The rural areas will have absolutely none, so you will need to carry more cash with you when you are out exploring. To keep your hands free while cycling or riding the bus, and your money safe, this may be a good time to use a money belt or another container that can be hidden in your clothing. Always tip the staff in cash, rather than adding a tip to a credit card receipt. The help relies on their tips, and cash tips can be utilized immediately. Although you don't have to tip, it is customary to do so in the larger cities. When you are eating in a country café, present your tip as a gift, giving it directly to the staff or family member with both hands to honor his or her service and say thank you for their food.

Of course, the next thing you'll need to be concerned with after eating a large meal is the restroom facilities. Unfortunately, they are not as modern and convenient as those in other more Westernized areas. Most toilets are of the squat variety, but if you stick to the larger hotels in the city, you can find the sit-down and flush type of toilet. Be sure to bring your own toilet paper and soap, since almost no place provides them.

There is also communal dining, both in the larger city cafes and in the country. This type of eating is where everyone is seated around a large pot of food or soup, and everyone dips into the same container. Some Westerners can be turned off by this type of eating, but you will be missing many conversations, fun, and some excellently spiced foods if you forego this adventure in eating. So, set your preconceived ideas aside and give it a try.

The following are the dates of some of the Cambodian holidays that were mentioned where you could enjoy food, fun, and the friendly company of the locals.

Khmer New Year	April 14th-17th
Ancestors' Day	September 19th-21st
Water Festival	November 2nd-6th

Like many of the sporting events all over the world, watching your favorite athletes compete is always accompanied by great food and drink. Cambodia observes these traditions as well. Regular affair when attending a kickboxing competition, football, or martial arts is to eat, drink, and make fools of yourselves. It's a time to let your hair down, shout support for your team, and be a real fan. Some of the best forms of Cambodian fast food can be found at these events, so don't hesitate to give them a taste.

Note: Remember that many of these holidays will be celebrated in Holy places, so please be respectful in your dress and manner. Cover yourself from shoulders to below knees and make sure you take off your shoes before entering temples and homes.

Chapter 4: Learning to Navigate — Cambodian Style

Navigating Cambodia is much different than that in many other countries, with its use of buses, Remoks, Cyclos, bicycles, kayaks, boats, trains, and cars. You would think these various modes of travel would be split, where some are used in the country and some in the city—but, not so much. Almost all types of transportation are used in every area, with the exception of water buffalo—you heard me! It is common to see water buffalo pulling carts in the country, but those are reserved for the rural travelers, most of whom are locals taking goods to the nearby village market.

If you wish to travel from Cambodia to one of the neighboring countries of Vietnam, Laos, or Thailand, the easiest way is by train. They run several times a day with times convenient for day trips or overnight stays. Traveling overland by train is such a beautiful way to see the country. If you are staying in Siem Reap or Phnom Penh, you'll want to make several stops to see the local sites as well, such as the world-famous Angkor temples. However, if you are going for a day trip, the best idea is to hire a Remok. We'll discuss those later.

For a two- to three-day trip from Angkor to Bangkok or Saigon, you'll pay as little as $40 to $60. If you want to travel by train from Siem Reap to Phnom Penh, you're looking at only $1.60. The buses and trains aren't the types piled with locals whose wares and belongings are hanging out every window and on top the transport. It's a clean, quick, and comfortable mode of travel where everybody keeps their individual space and you won't feel crowded or pushed from one destination to another or one seat to another.

Short Trips by Remoks

Remoks are Cambodia's version of a Tuk Tuk. They are open-air carriages that are powered by pedaling or by motors as well. You can hire these Remoks through your hotel, and they will pick you up, take you sight-seeing, and deliver your party back to the hotel for a very affordable price. The great thing about hiring a Remok is that the gentlemen driving them will speak English and because they are locals they know all the interesting and exciting places to visit. Most of the Remok tours last about four hours, but they can be scheduled for a full day if necessary. If you were staying in Siem Reap, a typical four-hour Remok tour might look something like this.

- Scheduled pick-up at your hotel in the morning.
- Travel to Angkor Wat to visit the incredible temples and all its splendor.
- Visit the Terrace of the Elephants.
- A stop for some refreshments, which would be polite to share with your Remok guide.
- Another stop at the Terrace of the Leper King.
- The last stop at the Bayon Temple.
- Then back to the hotel in the afternoon.

We'll describe some of these exotic destinations in a later chapter, but it would be a memorable day trip for very little expense—most less than $20.

Since many Remok drivers are competing for your business, they take pride in their vehicles. Most of them in the city are painted green, but those with a flair for marketing themselves will decorate their Remoks with vibrant colors and symbols that represent a variety of famous sites or Cambodian traditions. It's easy to see how they got the name "Remok," when you see what each letter means in the Khmer language. For example,

R = The "R" sets strong and comfortable on two legs, which represents power and strength.

E = The "E" has three equal branches of the same length, which represent fairness to the Cambodians. It also speaks of a willingness to learn and reach out to others.

M = The "M" represents stability and good character.

O = The "O" shows discipline.

K = The "K" shows tolerance and openness, a willingness to help others. It is also considered to be a letter of passion and dedication to the Cambodian culture.

A motorcycle or engine will power some of the larger Remoks and pull large groups, which will allow you to take your entire family together in the same Remok. Until you get out of the city, though, traveling by Remok can be an experience. In traffic, you will find yourself closing your eyes and saying a prayer as they weave in and out between bigger buses, cars, bicycles, Cyclos, and other Remok drivers. Everyone's in just as big a hurry to get to their planned sightseeing tours. Traffic lights are rare, and there are no designated lanes, so drivers are free to swing between other vehicles at random. So, take a deep breath and hang on to your seat, you're in for quite a ride.

Cyclos and Bicycles

These are more common on the outskirts of town, as they are powered by pedaling. The one disadvantage is that the Cyclo is limited to the number of people they carry. Some can transport only one person, and others can take two at a time. They are quieter and slower, so that might be the way to experience a short trip to the market or shops.

Bicycling your way into the countryside is an excellent way to get exercise and see the locals up close and personal. You can stop at your leisure and enjoy an entire day out on your own. Be sure to take water, though, as the weather is hot and humid. It can take the starch out of your sails if you're not used to it. Speaking of sails, there are also many modes of transportation that involve the rivers.

Exploring Cambodia by Boat or Kayak

With the Mekong River running through Cambodia, there are many types of boats from which to choose. You'll see very sleek, needle-like canoes that are painted beautifully and kept immaculate. You'll also see motorized canoes that are larger with raised planking to handle more people. Of the motorized variety, there are also boats of almost every size that resemble houseboats, steered by rudders and powered by engines that look and sound like small diesel lawnmowers. You won't see many kayaks until the river becomes significantly narrower and its waterways have given way to boats owned by local fishermen. Most the kayaks are for a single person and appeared to be a little wider than those you see in the States.

Although it is possible to kayak alone or with someone else in your party, many of the rivers have quite a current and could be dangerous for inexperienced kayakers. Even if you are familiar with handling a kayak, it's still beneficial to have a local guide so that you don't miss opportunities to see how the locals live. Some of the private guides live in the smaller villages and will often take you to their homes for a meal and a walking tour of the village. Of course, it is expected that you pay for both, but it can be an exciting excursion from the river trip. We'll talk later how you can kayak with the river dolphins—very cool!

If you are boating by yourself on the Mekong River, keep in mind that during or just after the wet season, the river is known to swell to four times its normal size. This also brings with it more river life and a stronger current to battle when rowing or paddling.

If you're feeling exceptionally adventurous, you might decide to take a water buffalo cart ride while in one of the more remote villages. Don't be frightened by their enormous horns and massive size; they are quite gentle and very well trained. They are so valuable to villagers that during times of celebration they are decorated and paraded around from village to village to pay homage to them and honor their hard work in the fields.

Whether you travel by land or by river, make sure to take some repellent with you, as the moisture and heat can attract some unpleasant hitchhikers. For this reason, if you have a choice, visiting Cambodia during the dry season is recommended and preferred.

We did not include particular train or bus schedules because the frequency and times with which they run are ever-changing, and the programs depend on where you are staying. Check with the hotel staff; they'll be able to refer the best modes of transportation at the most convenient times for the least amount of money.

Note: Hiking alone in the jungle is not recommended. Even hiking with a guide can be quite taxing, so be warned. There are horseback ventures that go into the forest, but only at safe distances—so if you want to do some bird-watching or perhaps see some wild jungle life, be sure to use a guide who is familiar with the terrain.

Note: If you hike the remote jungle, be sure also to wear the proper shoes. Although it can be physically challenging, you will get to see some untouched, less traveled places and visit some villages that some tourists never get to see. Some of Cambodia's most beautiful sites, animals, and people are those that live off the beaten paths.

Chapter 5: Destinations You Don't Want to Miss

The following are "must see" Cambodian places of cultural pride and national treasure. We have not listed them in any order of importance, as they are all equally beautiful and significant. Since many are Holy places, dress accordingly.

The Royal Palace of Phnom Penh

It was built in 1866 by the current King's great grandfather, His Majesty Preah Bat Norodom. The site of this golden beauty was chosen because it held great significance to the King, who was believed to be a direct descendent of the gods. It's splendor and magnificence do the gods proud, with its architectural style and rich design.

Within the Royal Throne Hall, there is a Silver Pagoda enclosure containing an Emerald Buddha statue made of Baccarat crystal and pure gold, weighing almost 200 pounds. It also includes 9,584 sparkling diamonds that demonstrate how they cherish Buddha. As you walk up the Italian marble steps and enter the throne room, you can't help but be dazzled by the 500 solid silver blocks, weighing over six tons.

Surrounding the Pagoda compound are hundreds of yards of murals called frescos, done in watercolors that depict Ramayana. Altogether, these murals make up the largest in all of South East Asia.

Angkor Wat

King Suryavarman II, reigning between 1131 and 1150, built the Angkor temple and dedicated it to the Hindu god, Vishnu. It took 30 years to build, and it features the longest, continuous bas-relief in the world. Bas-relief is a type of sculpting done on a wall of the same material, which makes the figures look as though they are coming out from the wall itself. The bas-relief at Angkor Wat tells the stories of Hindu mythology with elegant beauty and scenic detail.

Angkor Wat is often referred to as the heart and soul of Cambodia, and it's easy to see why as you walk its causeway to approach the ancient sandstone fortress. These massive sandstone blocks were excavated from the Holy mountain of Phnom Kulen nearly 32 miles away. Raft transported each block down the Siem Reap River. It is estimated that thousands of people, as well as 6,000 elephants, worked endlessly to complete Angkor Wat.

The compound was designed to replicate the Hindu thought of Yuga or the four ages. Visitors who walk the causeway and enter through the front gates into the large courtyards and on to the last tower are said to have metaphorically gone through time back to the first age of universal creation. As you travel this reverent pathway, you will see many locks of hair along the way. These have been left by young couples preparing to marry or people as a show of giving thanks to the gods for their good fortune.

There is absolutely nothing like Angkor Wat in the modern world. As you leave this awesome place, you'll take its powerful beauty and strength home with you as a remembrance of Cambodia.

The Massive and Twisted Trees of Ta Prohm

Although the temple has fallen into ruin, its beauty is preserved by the twisted trees that have fingered their way through the massive fallen stones and the enormous statues carved into the walls. Some of the temple features look as though they were carved into the trees, rather than the other way around. Everywhere you look, you'll see faces peeking between tree roots that are bigger around than a house, and partial bodies of gods wrapped by the webbed roots climbing all the way up the walls of the temple to free themselves in the sky above. It's a magical sight, and one wonders whether the ruins were planned by the gods to look as they do.

The Terrace of the Elephants

King Jayavarman VII built the structure in the 12th century. For as far as the eye can see, carved elephants are looking as though they are coming through a wall that is longer than the length of three football fields. The trunks of these elephants hang down to the ground to form giant pillars. Atop this great wall is a terrace from which the King would stand over his court each day to hear and resolve the problems of its citizens. Various sculptures on the inner walls include carvings of a horse with many heads, chariot races, and elephants with their riders engaged in hunts, as well as the ever-present Buddha.

The Terrace of the Leper King

Quite close to The Terrace of the Elephants is The Terrace of the Leper King. It was named after a sculpture that was discovered at the site that depicts the Hindu god, Yama, which is the god of Death. With the extreme humidity and heat of Cambodia, moss grew over the statue, making it look as if it had leprosy with the moss that trailed its face. Because these marks reminded the people of a Cambodian legend of an Angkorian King who had leprosy, it was named the Terrace of the Leper King.

The Ghost Town at Bokor Hill

A remnant of Cambodia's darkest days is the Ghost Town at Bokor Hill. It was built by the French Colonials and included a hotel that's grandeur would rival any you'd find in France, a large casino, a small church, a post office, and several boutiques. Thousands of Cambodians were forced into slave labor, dying in the heat so the wealthy French could continue to live in the style of their homeland. Most of the town was built in the early 1900s, and by the 1940s was abandoned when the over-taxed Cambodians stood against them. The once beautiful buildings are now abandoned and left to ruin as the dense jungle comes to claim her own once again.

Although there are no roads that are travel worthy that go into the town, for you independent adventurers, you'll enjoy the mysterious quiet and fallen grandeur of the colonial Queens' nest atop Bokor Hill.

The Beaches of Sihanoukville

Cambodia boasts some of the most pristine, clear water, white sandy beaches in the world. Their names are as intriguing as their scenery, with Independence and Victory Beaches as well as Serendipity Beach, and these are just to name a few. The small town of Sihanoukville has very little to offer in the way of fancy nightlife or five-star hotels, but its beaches are five-star quality for sure. Most of the beaches are not densely populated, and there are small thatched eateries that offer a grilled fare of fish and fruit. Of course, there is always the refreshing smoothie to cool you during an afternoon of lazy beach time.

The waters are so clear you can see the bottom rocks and sand until the water gets so deep that the dark blue hue of the water covers its hidden treasures. There are boats to take you over to the island where you can snorkel and dive to your heart's content, and then have an easy meal on one of its many beaches. Sokha Beach does have Cambodia's first five-star hotel with a private beach. You can expect there'll be even more where that came from in the future. All this is only a 45-minute flight or a 5-hour taxi ride from Phnom Penh.

Ream National Park

Not far from Sihanoukville is Ream National Park, which is one of the most beautiful sites of Cambodia. Until a few years ago, this region was isolated and unspoiled, so you'll be seeing it in its infancy. Along with a genuine Cambodian temple, it has "Jurassic Park" like waterfalls, numerous species of birds to watch, and safari tours that take you through the dense jungle to the mountains that overlook the sunny beaches of Sihanoukville. It's only about 11 miles from Sihanoukville, so you'll want to include it in your tour of sun worshiping on one of Sihanoukville's clean white beaches.

Playing with the River Dolphins

Taking a Remok or Tuk Tuk from Kratie to Kampi will cost you under $20, and the experience will be one in a million. With about

100 friendly river dolphins, you're sure to see one if you can take your eyes off the incredible golden sunsets. The dolphins are friendly and quite playful, eager to show visitors their silly antics as they fly through the water of the Mekong River. They'll swim circles around your slow-going boat, peaking their heads up at you to get a look and give a nod hello. It's obvious that the Dolphins are just as entertained by us as we are by them. You just can't help but giggle as you experience them skimming along the top of the water acting as some of the best little ambassadors of Cambodia.

Mondulkiri Province

Although most people stay in one of Cambodia's larger cities, you won't want to miss seeing the quaint mountain village of Mondulkiri Province, with its intimate setting and authentic Cambodian culture. Those living in Mondulkiri Province still carry on the traditions of their ancestors, so you'll feel as though you're stepping back into a Cambodian lifestyle that is rarely witnessed in the more modern cities. Its' people wear continuous smiles and eagerly wave at any newcomers to their villages. Visiting Mondulkiri Province will give you a time to reflect and enjoy the peace and tranquility of its surrounding mountains and dense jungle.

There is so much to see and do in Cambodia, and whether you're feasting on their food or their ancient attractions, it's almost more than you can take in during a brief holiday. The sheer beauty of Cambodia is only rivaled by the gentle spirit of its people.

Chapter 6: Celebrating Today's Cambodia

It is right that we celebrate the strength and resolve of the Cambodian people, who have been through so much upheaval. Through it all, they remain a gentle, unassuming society. The dangers of the Cambodian culture are that its people leave themselves open to being politically bullied by powerful, aristocratic government officials, which has happened throughout history.

Even though the political situation has changed and the big cities are looking more modern, most of rural Cambodia remains its unspoiled self. The villages are still mostly agricultural, family-oriented communities where everyone knows everybody else and people care for their neighbors. The rice fields are still being plowed by water buffalo, the gentle giants of old-time Cambodia. It's difficult for us to see Cambodia ever being a country where the old has been forgotten, thank goodness.

The same goes for the older people of Cambodia. Instead of being disregarded as in many other modern societies, Cambodia remains a country that honors its aged. Their youth value their input and welcome their voice, which gives us outsiders cause to pause and consider what we might be missing in the resources of our older generations.

The wonderful thing about repeat visits to Cambodia is that you know that you can return to the same things that you loved about Cambodia during your last visit. You know that there will still be more ruins to explore, more temples to visit, more exotic cuisine to taste, and more friendly people are waiting to welcome you to their beautiful country.

Americans often worry about how people in different countries will receive us, but there's no reason to be anxious when visiting Cambodia. They speak our language, eagerly forgive our social faux pas, and show us another way of life that values everyone equally. Not that there are some things to overcome in Cambodia, such as crowded marketplaces and crazy traffic, but in the scheme of things, those are minor issues. It's a world so different from our own that we're challenged not to stand in public with our mouths gaping open in disbelief.

Many people who have traveled to Cambodia would not have thought of it as an exciting and intriguing vacation spot before having gone. However, once the Cambodian people have opened their homes and hearts to you, all you can think of when leaving is when you will be returning.

Even though most of the citizens of Cambodia live on less than a dollar a day, you don't look at them as people in poverty. Instead, you see the richness of their culture and the abundance of their relationships. You don't see the insecurity and need, but rather the quiet confidence of a happy society. You don't see starving and neglected children, but rather happy villagers who are playing traditional games and sharing celebratory feasts. Perhaps it's the Cambodian magic that blankets your eyes to all things unpleasant.

With all the wars and genocide of Cambodia's past, they now have one of the youngest populations in the world, with sixty percent or more being under the age of thirty. It will be interesting to see how their views and experiences will change the face of Cambodia. Will they continue to preserve the past, perhaps even being trapped by the flaws that enslaved Cambodians in the early 1900s? Or, will they put forth a new force, a new resolve to be a people to be reckoned with in the Asian world? With the young come new ideas and values, which might create quite a difference in these next few decades for Cambodia.

Much of the success of Cambodia's future will depend on these young workers. Will they become skilled in trade and up–to–date in technology? Will they join forces with emerging Asian nations and benefit from their prosperity, but be held down by their power? One thing you can be certain of is that Cambodia's burgeoning tourist trade will help to turn that around and bring them into the 21st century. It's acknowledged that tourism plays an important part in the financial stability of Cambodia, and they will work hard to promote and develop that industry. There are a lot of positives to be said about the Cambodian culture, and one of them is that they are hard-working, resourceful people.

The traditions and customs will stay, but beneath the surface of a youthful population will be a need to create strength and well-being for their people. All these plausible changes could mean higher prices for travel and accommodations, so there's no time like the present to enjoy the wonders of Cambodia.

Conclusion:

Thank you again for downloading this book!

I hope this book was able to help you understand the history and culture of Cambodia and its people. There are many national treasures and ancient sites to see in Cambodia, that it is impossible to describe them all, but perhaps we have whet your appetite to see what makes Cambodia one of the most exciting places to visit. By reading our book, we hope you have learned things about the Cambodian people that will help you to respect their customs and traditions as you travel within their borders. Most of all, we hope you will take our book with you and refer to if often for any questions you might have or additional information you might need.

When you visit a faraway land, it's not all about what you see and learn while you're there, but the memories and lessons you bring back home. We wanted to open your eyes to ideas and beliefs that you could borrow and apply them to your life upon your return. Cambodia is a memorable place, a colorful, diverse, country that has been influenced by so many other nations it will be as if you are visiting all of Asia in one trip.

The next step is to prepare for your trip and pack your bags. Don't forget to consult your travel advisory for environmental conditions and weather. It's better to get your money exchanged before your trip so that you're well-prepared with small bills to take care of your immediate needs once you get off the plane. Whether it's the wet or dry season in Cambodia, you can count on it being hot and humid, so pack your clothes accordingly, with a few extras to visit the Holy Temples and Royal Palace.

As you prepare for your trip to Cambodia, you might want to consider taking some small gifts with you for the people with whom you will share a meal and enjoy the company of them and their families. Gifts from another country are always exciting, and it will give them an idea of where you're from and a view of your culture. It doesn't have to be anything elaborate, just a small token of your appreciation for their hospitality.

A friend of mine took coloring books and markers for the children and beautifully decorated stationary and pens for the women. For the men, she took a calendar with photos of places in the states. The items were all flat and easy to pack, taking up very little space. However, when given to the villagers, their faces revealed their pleasure at receiving gifts that were brought from such a faraway land and ones that revealed their visitors' way of life. Giving the gifts was nothing compared to what was given in return — genuine warmth and appreciation.

We hope we've given you travel ideas that will appeal to everyone in the family, no matter the age or gender. From visiting the ruins to laying in hammocks on the beach, it's a world that you can lose yourself in without too much effort or anxiety. If you're looking forward to seeing the wildlife, make sure to bring your binoculars as well. You'll be amazed at what you can see as you take a guided hike through the jungles or to the top of the mountains.

If you have enjoyed our book, keep your eyes open for other similar travel guides in the future. We also ask you for one more favor. Would you be kind enough to leave a review for this book on Amazon? It'd be greatly appreciated!

Thank you, and good luck to you in all your adventures!

Printed in Great Britain
by Amazon